GOD'S *Concerned* ABOUT WHAT CONCERNS *Me*

A DAILY WALK WITH THE FATHER

SHARONETTE SMART
JAMILLA S. ROBERTSON

Printed in the United States of America
ISBN: 978-1-7349160-8-9
Library of Congress Cataloging-in-Publication Data

Graphics & Marketing: SHERO Publishing & Greenlight Creations
Graphics Designs - glightcreations.com/ glightcreations@gmail.com

Creative Book Cover Design: Jamain Freeman for Freeman Multimedia
freemanmultimedia.com ~ jamain@freemanmultimedia.com

Initial Book Formatting and Logistics-Yvette Hawke
Final Book Layout- SHERO Publishing

shero publishing

getpublished@sheropublishing.com

S H E R O P U B L I S H I N G . C O M

Table Of Contents

From The Heart of The Father...

My Beloved Daughter,

From creation you were the apple of my eye. My care of you was such, that I didn't form you from the dust of the earth; but I caused a deep sleep to come upon the man Adam, and from his rib, you were created. I invested so much creativity in your creation. From the forming of your breast, to the curve in your spine; from the curves in your hips that flowed into your thighs. Your face, your lips, your smile, your eyes; you were wonderfully and beautifully created, you were my wonderful design. In my image and after my likeness were you made; dominion over everything was the power to you I gave. Power to tread on serpents, scorpions, the like, and such. This power I gave to you, because I love you so much. You, my Daughter, are dearly beloved, it is your creation I'm most proud of. This letter I dedicate to you because I wanted you to know, the love I have for you, you can never out grow. You're Daddy's Girl.

Always,
Your Father

This Daily Walk With God...

Was birthed in uncertain times; 2020 COVID-19 pandemic, and a world uprooted by racial inequality, which gave life to the BLM Movement (Black Lives Matter). These are truly unprecedented times, uncertain times, confusing times, challenging times, mourning times and fearful times. These times have not only challenged and stretched our faith; in some cases, they have caused many of us to question our faith. Is God listening? Does He really care? Can't He see what's happening? Will He intervene? The impact of this Corona Virus is devastating; the racial injustice and divide has taken one too many lives. "Lord, help us," we cry, we pray. God has the power to deliver us, to make this all go away. People are dying by the thousands. I mean thousands are globally dying every day. Inside my heart I can hear the Father say...

"***If my people, which are called by my name, would humble themselves and pray, and seek my face, and turn from their wicked ways; then will I hear from heaven, and will forgive their sins, and will heal their land." 2 Chron. 7:14***

GOD IS LISTENING FOR A SOUND

What sound? I'm glad you asked. God is listening for the sound of the repentant church, according to ***2 Chronicles 7:14.*** You see, that passage wasn't written to the world, it was written to the church, to God's chosen people. You and I, we are the church, we are God's chosen people. He's talking to us. This was God's response to Solomon who was praying on behalf of the children of Israel, "God's chosen people" in the previous chapter ***(2 Chronicles 6)***.

In 2 Chronicles 7:12-13 God says this to Solomon, ***"If I shut up heaven that there be no rain, or if I command the locusts to devour the land, or if I send pestilence among my people;"*** Then he goes on to say in verse fourteen, ***" If my people, which are called by my name, would humble themselves and pray, and seek my face, and turn from their wicked ways; then will I hear from heaven, and will forgive their sins, and will heal their land."*** In verses 12-13 God is saying to Solomon that if I, God, not the devil, not the president, not the conspiracy theorists, but if I cause all these things to happen and my people

REPENT and TURN from their wicked, sinful ways, then He would hear from heaven, forgive our sins, and heal our land. God is listening for a sound of a REPENTANT CHURCH! It is our prayer that these next 31 days spent in this daily devotion will bring us all to the place of repentance, releasing the sound that God desires to hear so that He will heal our land. No, we will never go back to life as we knew it because God is desiring and He is doing a new thing in the earth. Our response to what He's doing is to trust Him by faith. Take this journey with us as we seek to become the people of God He's ordained us to be. And, when we line up with the word and will of God for our lives, the world will benefit from us getting in position. Take the journey, you have nothing to lose and new life to gain. Remember, God wants to do a new thing, in us. Yes, He wants to do a new thing in you. We'll never be the same, for He calls us His Daughters.

DAY ONE

I GET IT FROM MY FATHER
MY D.N.A.

One of the worst things that can happen to a little girl, is that she's born into a fatherless situation. She often lacks validation, affirmation, and value. Her self-worth, self-esteem, and self- image are often molded and defined by the lack of the love, steering, and rearing of her father. She finds herself searching and often settling; trying to compensate for the void his absence left in her life. The parallel thing about both of their lives is; often times, the absent father is the son of an absent father. Therefore, the cycle of life repeats itself. Yet, today your life has a different caption, you, my queen sister, are the daughter of the Most High God. When you said yes to Jesus, you said "yes" to the D.N.A. of God, the Dominion, Nature, and Authority of God . You were made in the image and likeness of God according to **(Gen. 1:26)**. You, have dominion over everything that exists according to **(Gen. 1:28)**. So, as you embrace this day, embrace it like the royalty you are. Your self-worth should be *on fleek* today, knowing you have dominion over the fish of the sea, and over the fowl of the air, and over every living thing that moveth upon the earth. Knowing that you, yes you, have the power within you to nurture life within. You, my dear, have creative, producing power. The atmosphere must conform to your very word, **Let there be**, and watch it come to pass. You got the power!

Your D.N.A. gives you access to the Kingdom, to your daddy's bank account. To His sphere of influence. So from this day forward my queen sister, adjust your crown. No longer will your head hang down. You are a royal priesthood, a chosen generation. The apple of your daddy's eye. Look up and live. Your best days are your latter days. As you maneuver throughout your day, remember our father has already paved the way, we win! No matter what it looks like, we WIN! Allow the prayer, meditation scripture, and affirmation focus be your guiding force on today.

PRAYER:

Dear Father, It's Me________ (Put Your Name Here) I come to You today confessing my sins, my short comings, and my faults. I confess, that due to my lack of knowledge of my true D.N.A., I have lived beneath my privilege. Today I reclaim my birth right, I walk in the **D**ominion, **N**ature, and **A**uthority given to me from the foundation of the world, from whence ever the world was created, I am. In Jesus Name. Amen.

SCRIPTURE FOCUS: *Genesis 1:26*

"And God Said, Let us make man in our image, after our likeness: and let them have dominion over the fish of the sea, and over the fowl of the air, and over the cattle, and over every creeping thing that creepeth upon the earth."

AFFIRMING FOCUS:

I am made in the image and likeness of God. I walk affirmed in the **D**ominion, **N**ature, and **A**uthority He has given to me.

MY SPACE FOR REFLECTING

(IT IS WRITTEN)

DAY TWO

A WORTHY SACRIFICE

We have all heard of the story of Cain and Able, the first two heirs born to Adam and Eve. We know that Abel was a keeper of the sheep, and Cain was a tiller of the ground. The bible declares that Cain brought of the fruit of the ground, (he literally threw an offering together and offered it unto the Lord), whereas Able was intentional with his offering unto the Lord, so much so that he not only brought of the first born of the flock, but he brought the best of the firstborn. Able rendered unto God a worthy sacrifice. The best of the firstborn, not just any ole offering. The bible says Cain brought of the fruit of the ground. He just gathered something up to give to God, there was no thought to his selection. He wasn't intentional about the produce, he brought to God. God had respect for Able's offering **(Gen. 4:1-7)**. Are you rendering unto God a worthy sacrifice? Is your prayer life intentional? Are you guilty of only praying when you have a need? When you're in trouble? Is God pleased with your sacrifice of worship? Are you intentionally setting aside time to spend in His presence? A worthy sacrifice is one that is intentional. That is purposed in one's heart. One that you gave great thought and consideration to. It's not the quantity of your sacrifice that gets

God attention, but it's the quality of your sacrifice. Did you randomly decide to pray, **(Not that anything is wrong with having a random conversation with your Father)**, but that's not a worthy sacrifice, that's not intentionally adjusting your life, your schedule to make time to spend in the presence of God. Did you just randomly put a dollar in the offering, **(Not that anything is wrong with putting a dollar in the offering, if that's the best that you can do)**, but, if you paid all your bills first, got your hair and nails done, a new outfit for Mother's Day, and then decided to bring God a portion of what's leftover; that's not a worthy sacrifice. God desires a worthy sacrifice. Will you give it today?

PRAYER:

Dear Father, I ask that You forgive me, for I acknowledge that I have not always rendered a worthy sacrifice unto You. I haven't been intentional about setting aside time to spend in Your presence. I consecrate my prayer life to You Lord. I know I haven't put You first in my money, but today all of that changes. Today I put You first, surrendering to You a worthy sacrifice! In Jesus Name. Amen.

SCRIPTURE FOCUS: Genesis 4:1-7

"And Abel, he also brought of the firstlings of his flock and the fat thereof. And the Lord had respect unto Abel and to his offering;"

AFFIRMING FOCUS:

It's not how much time I spend in prayer, that makes it a worthy sacrifice, it's being intentional about spending time in prayer. Setting aside an appointed time. Being intentional and purposeful about all I surrender unto God. Today I surrender to You a worthy sacrifice.

MY SPACE FOR REFLECTING

(IT IS WRITTEN)

DAY THREE

GIVING GOD MY YES

Can you remember a time when someone asked you to do them a favor? Because of who it was, your immediate response was YES! You started the task only to discover that it was more complex than you ever intended it to be. When we confess our salvation to the Lord, we are saying "YES" to Him. We openly confess that, yes we need a Savior. We realize that Jesus IS exactly who He says He is. The Messiah, the Son of God, the one who is able to do all things and has all power. Our YES to Him is a matter of the heart as well as the mouth. When we tell Him "YES" we are submitting an exchange. We forsake our will for His. We invite the Holy Spirit in to do inventory of our hearts and ask Him to clean the areas of our lives that have and are causing the most damage to us. Whether it takes a moment, a month, year, or a lifetime, our YES to the Lord will challenge us to step out of ourselves to achieve the greatness that He has predestined for us from the beginning. When we tell our Heavenly Father YES, we have no idea of all that our YES will entail. Yet we want to hear, "Well done, thy good and faithful servant" when we arrive at the gates of Heaven. The Holy Spirit dwells among us leading and guiding us to accomplish His tasks here on Earth.

Surrendering and submitting ourselves to the Lord only furthers our YES with Him. We are not our own, we've been bought with a hefty price that we can never repay. We surrender and obey Him even when it doesn't make sense. His word confirms over and over that all of His promises are YES and amen.

PRAYER:

Dear Father, Today I give You my YES! Yes to Your Will and to Your Way. I confess with my mouth that Jesus Christ is Lord, and I believe in my heart that You, Father, have raised Him from the dead. According to Your word I am saved. My YES is sealed in the blood of Jesus Christ! I say Yes Lord YES! In Jesus Name. Amen.

SCRIPTURE FOCUS: Galatians 2:20 - "I have been crucified with Christ and I no longer live, but Christ lives in me. The life I now live in the body, I live by faith in the Son of God, who loved me and gave himself for me."

AFFIRMING FOCUS:

Today my life changes forever! Today I say, "YES" to God. I surrender. I want to know You more. I surrender. Not my will, or what I want. Your Will is what I want! I give You my YES!

MY SPACE FOR REFLECTING

(IT IS WRITTEN)

DAY FOUR

I JUST WANT TO PLEASE MY DAD

I can remember when I had a brief employment with a local fast food restaurant. During my training, the owner's son had graduated from college and started in the restaurant as well. When he first started, he was extremely excited at the thought that one day he would run the company. Over time, he began to look overwhelmed at how much information he would have to retain. I simply asked him, "Is this what you really want to do with your life?" He paused and stated back to me, "I just want to please my dad!" From that moment on, regardless of how frustrated he appeared, he overcame every obstacle and every challenge. He completed every task set before him. As passionate as he was about pleasing his natural father, we should be equally passionate about pleasing our Heavenly Father. The only way we can do that is to develop a personal and intimate relationship with Him. The more we pray and study His word, the more we will develop characteristic traits that display Him more and more. To please Him means to come into agreement with what He has already said about us. There is nothing we can do, per say, to make Him happy. His love for us is already to the max, so to "please" Him will never involve any type of emotion. We are totally and completely accepted. He is pleased by our faith, fearing Him, being spiritually minded, and obeying Him.

PRAYER:

Dear Father,

I come into agreement with everything You have spoken concerning me, by my doing so, I know this pleases You. As I seek You the more, I am confident that I grow in grace, the more I seek Your face. I only desire to please You Father. In Jesus Name. Amen.

SCRIPTURE FOCUS: Hebrews 11:6 - "And without faith it is impossible to please God, because anyone who comes to him must believe that he exists and that he rewards those who earnestly seek him."

AFFIRMING FOCUS:

Today, Father, I agree with everything You say about me. I realize pleasing You is not about my emotions, but about my faith. I continue to walk in faith, and not by sight, to please You.

MY SPACE FOR REFLECTING

(IT IS WRITTEN)

DAY FIVE

COURAGE FOR THE JOURNEY

The daily cares and uncertainties of life have caused many to flee and retreat. To give in to the fear tactics of the enemy. Although life is happening to me, in this will I be confident, what the Lord has begun in my life doesn't end here. God has a plan. I confess out loud, **"I ain't over!"** Sometimes the valleys in life can make one feel as if we walk alone, but I am encouraged, because **(Joshua 1:9)** reminds me that God is with me wherever I go. I fear no evil, the Lord is with me. The journey seems long and the way sometimes hard, but I am strong and courageous. Through roadblocks, set-ups, setbacks and betrayals, the Lord is with me. Through layoffs, cutoffs, and delays, I have the blessed assurance that the delay is not a denial. When life throws us lemons, we must be resourceful and open a lemonade stand. When fear comes to grip us, our faith must take a stand. As I reflect on **Joshua 1:9**, it may be scary when walking through unknown territory, when having to conquer something you have never encountered before. We don't go alone, but our confidence in God is with us wherever we go, and whatever we go through; we have only to be strong and courageous. I challenge you on today my sister, as you read, and embrace day five, take courage for your journey ahead.

Know that the Spirit of God will never lead you where the power of God can't keep you. He goes before us and prepares the way. He takes the journey with us, so come what may. Look at your storm, your test, your story, and repeat after me, "I've got the courage for my journey!"

PRAYER:

Dear Father,

I put my courage and trust in only you. I can accomplish all things, there is nothing I can't do. The blessed assurance of Your presence through the valley and the shadow of death, I will fear no evil for Thou art with me whithersoever I go. In Jesus Name. Amen.

SCRIPTURE FOCUS: Joshua 1:9- "Have not I commanded thee? Be strong and of a good courage; be not afraid, neither be thou dismayed; for the Lord thy God is with thee whithersoever thou goest."

AFFIRMING FOCUS:

You don't have to have all the answers. You don't even have to have the road map. Just know that God is always with you, so take courage in that.

MY SPACE FOR REFLECTING

(IT IS WRITTEN)

DAY SIX

THE GPS SYSTEM OF GOD

The first navigation system existed over 2000 years ago. In **Genesis 12:1-3** God tells Abraham, **"Get thee out of thy country, and from thy kindred, and from thy father's house, unto a land that I will shew thee: And I will make of thee a great nation, and I will bless thee, and make thy name great; and thou shalt be a blessing: And I will bless them that bless thee, and curse him that curseth thee; and in thee shall all families of the earth be blessed."** Abraham had no knowledge of where he was going, but he was submitted to God, he trusted God. So he left what was familiar and followed the leading, guidance, and direction of the Spirit of God. At seventy-five years old, Abraham was venturing out in faith, trusting the leading of God, without the aid of Siri, Google Maps, OnStar, or any other navigation system. God had given Abraham clear directives as to what he should do, and without question he gathered his family and he followed the voice and leading of God. In this life we will have to be willing to forsake all others and follow Christ. The GPS **(God's Provisional System)** of God, is powered by the Holy Spirit. If we yield to it, follow and obey it like Abraham, we will find our place of promise. You see Abraham was led to a land of promise and provision. The favor of God was upon him so much so that even his nephew Lot followed him when he left home. He recognized the blessing on Abraham's life and he wasn't going to be left out. The blessing of Abraham is on you and I. The word of God declares that the seed of Abraham would be blessed. That's us! We are blessed! There will be people who may try to attach themselves to us because, they too see the favor on our lives. There may be those places God wants to transition us from. The question is, will you follow the leading of God? Will you go where He leads you without question, like Abraham did? When we ask God to take the wheel, we must be willing to surrender the keys. We can't sit in the passenger and driver seat. We must trust the GPS navigation system of God. The promise land awaits you.

PRAYER:

Dear Father,

Where You lead me I will follow. Where You lead me I will go. Lead me Father, Lord I trust You, Lead me where so-ever I go. Order my steps Lord in Your word, will, and way. In Jesus Name. Amen.

SCRIPTURE FOCUS: Proverbs 3:5-6 - "Trust in the Lord with all thine heart; and lean not unto thine own understanding. In all thy ways acknowledge him, and he will direct thy paths."

AFFIRMING FOCUS:

The GPS navigation system of God will never lead you where He can't sustain you. Trust the Lord to order your steps. He's ordained your destination.

MY SPACE FOR REFLECTING

(IT IS WRITTEN)

DAY SEVEN

FINISH IT

I've always been told, "Whatever you do, do with all of your might. Things that are done half, are never done right." When God calls us to do anything, He doesn't expect us to do it halfway. We sometimes hesitate on completing the task because we don't feel qualified or even worthy that He would entrust an assignment to us. Not only is it important that we start the task, but it is equally important to finish the task. It doesn't take faith to start, it takes faith to finish. We often allow various situations, circumstances, people, and distractions to steer us away from completing the simplest tasks. Time is short. God has gifted us with every ability needed to complete anything. It's up to us to tap into the wealth of knowledge He provides for us. Finishing anything requires commitment. Think of a marathon. It takes time and preparation for a race of such magnitude. Many start the journey of the marathon, but many find themselves dropping out before getting to the finish line. Commitment to completing an assignment requires dedication. It comes from the core of your heart that you are determined even when the odds are stacked up against us. Think of the many people in the Bible that were given various assignments; Moses, Noah, Joshua, Paul, Ester, and

Nehemiah, just to name a few. They all had pretty difficult assignments from God, but they all completed them, through every challenge, and God's plan prevailed. Regardless of the size of the assignment, it is our responsibility to pray, listen for His voice, seek His direction, and carry them out with the help of the Holy Spirit. After all, it's all for His glory! Nothing we do outside of God matters anyway. It is what we do for Christ that will last. If God called you to it, He has well equipped you for it. The provision for the vision, for the assignment, has already been prepared for us. We must start and commit to complete the task. It's not always easy to complete what we started, life will happen. We must commit not to quit! You have what it takes, SO FINISH IT!

PRAYER:

Dear Father,

I acknowledge the greatest finished work was completed on Calvary, with the sacrifice of Your Son Jesus Christ. Just as he stayed the course to complete the assignment given to him, it is my desire to do the same. Today I commit not to quit, and to complete every assignment and every task I set out to do. It is finished. In Jesus Name. Amen.

SCRIPTURE FOCUS: Philippians 1:6

" Being confident of this very thing, that he which have begun a good work in you will perform it until the day of Jesus Christ."

AFFIRMING FOCUS:

Today I commit to FINISH! I will finish every assignment and every task. I will give it my all, I will do my best. Giving in and giving up is a thing of the past. I will finish what I start, whether I'm first, or I'm last, I WILL FINISH!

MY SPACE FOR REFLECTING

(IT IS WRITTEN)

DAY EIGHT

I KNOW YOU BEST

We are constantly surrounded by family, friends, and love ones who know us. They sometimes tend to see things in us that we haven't necessarily seen in ourselves. They know our flaws, our strengths, our mannerisms because we've spent so much time around them. We can say that we know them in the same manner. We often look at God as being someone that may know us, but we struggle in believing that we could come to know Him in that way. For some reason we think He is too vast for us to know Him on an intimate level. Our Father is the creator of all things and there will always be something new that we will discover about Him, but that doesn't mean we can't get to know Him in the most intimate way. Just like our loves ones, the more time we spend with Him in prayer, His word, and worship, the more He reveals himself to us and communicate things to us about Him, even about ourselves that we had no idea was even possible to know. We often let the word "intimate" intimidate us to believing that we could not have an intimate relationship with God. Intimacy, in this sense, is not associated with sex. An intimate relationship with God is more about sharing. God shared His best with us when He sent His son Jesus in the flesh to the earth. Jesus understood and experienced every emotion that we have ever dealt with. When we are intimate with someone, we have a level of trust with them. We share many of our deepest and darkest secrets with them. Well, when we trust Jesus, we can share ourselves in the same manner. The more we share with Him, the more He shares himself with us. After all, if we want to know how a particular thing works, we would refer to the instructions or the manufacturer. To fully understand why we even exist, for what reason we were created, and how we can live a more fulfilled life in Him, we must refer back to OUR manufacturer. After all, He does know us the best!

PRAYER:

Dear Father,

I take comfort in knowing You know me better than anyone, better than I even know myself. So today I release all my inhibitions; I release my fears, and cares. I trust You with my life, for You Lord have numbered even my very hairs. You know me best. In Jesus Name. Amen.

SCRIPTURE FOCUS: Luke 12:7

"But even the very hairs of your head are all numbered. Fear not therefore: ye are of more value than many sparrows."

AFFIRMING FOCUS:

He knows Me. He's knows me best. He knows me. He knows me better than the rest. He knows me; and despite all that He knows, He loves me!

MY SPACE FOR REFLECTING

(IT IS WRITTEN)

DAY NINE

WHAT SOURCE ARE YOU DRAWING FROM?

A common way to obtain water is from a well. It's basically a hole in the ground held open by pipe and attached to a pump. The pump is what draws the water up for use. Many factors play a part to ensure the well effectively supplies water to the source that's drawing from it; such as the location, the actual construction, and the pumping system. Once these factors are established, maintenance is required on a regular basis to keep the well functioning properly. Occasionally wells can run dry, and the pump may be pumping nothing but air. A solution to this problem would be to lower the pump further down, to ensure it remains beneath the water level, so the well doesn't have that problem anymore. Just as the well serves a major function in a house to supply water throughout, The Holy Spirit is necessary to provide living water that will never run out. Jesus promised that the living waters of the Holy Spirit will flow out of our bellies when we come to drink from the living water Jesus provides. When we come to Christ and drink, (continuous communication with him, having faith, loving others as he loves us, pray, and seek Him through his word), the spirit flows from us and gives our spirit life. People draw from a well to quench a thirst, cook, wash clothes, etc. We expect the water to flow when the faucet is turned on. The problem comes in when the faucet is turned on and nothing comes out. Spiritually, our living water, the Holy Spirit, is always available, always plentiful within believers. Through faith we can all receive the same spirit. We can draw from the same well of living water that will never run dry. We may draw from the living water for many reasons; strength, comfort, forgiveness, or reconciliation, but nevertheless The Holy Spirit is deep enough, huge enough, and so eternal, that when the enemy wants to make us think we are running dry, we can be replenished.

PRAYER:

Dear Father,

I come thirsty. An empty cup before a full fountain. Fill me Lord with Your Holy Spirit. I empty out myself before You Oh Lord, less of me and more of You, until there's none of me and all of You is my prayer. In Jesus Name. Amen.

SCRIPTURE FOCUS: John 4:14 "But whosoever drinketh of the water that I shall give him shall never thirst; but the water that I shall give him shall be in him a well of water springing up into everlasting life."

AFFIRMING FOCUS:

Fill my cup Lord. I lift it up Lord. Fill this thirsting in my soul; make me complete, make me whole. I am empty without You.

MY SPACE FOR REFLECTING

(IT IS WRITTEN)

DAY TEN

GET OUT YOUR FEELINGS

Have you ever said or done something in haste? Have your emotions or feelings ever led you astray? The thing about feelings is that they are so unpredictable. One moment you can be happy enjoying your life, in the same space something can happen, or you get a call that transforms your whole day. I was on social media one day and I heard ***Desiree G. Briggs*** say something that stuck with me, she said, ***"One bad moment does not make a bad day."*** I thought this was a profound statement. I heard, "Get out your feelings!" It had so much revelation in it. We have the tendency to allow a moment in time to derail our whole day. Something someone said or did can be a trigger for us. For some of us, these events could have taken place years ago, but something presently happens and it triggers a feeling, an emotion. If we aren't careful and learn how to manage these feelings and emotions, we can literally be the cause of us missing out on opportunities, blessings, promotions, relationships that were intended to bless you. This reminds me of a story in the Bible found in the 15th chapter of Matthew where a mother went to Jesus for help for her daughter who was vexed with a devil. She asked Jesus to have mercy on her daughter, then he told her, ***"It is not meet to take***

the children's bread, and to cast it to dogs" she replied, ***"Truth, Lord: yet the dogs eat of the crumbs which fall from their master's table."*** Now, let's be honest if Jesus had called you a Dog, would this have been your response? Would it be accurate to say that the cameras from TMZ would have been rolling, along with reporters from the Shade Room. Yet, after her response Jesus said, ***"O woman, great is thy faith: be it unto thee even as thou wilt."*** From that very hour her daughter was made whole. This mother did not get in her feelings. She did not allow her emotions to cause her to miss out on the miracle her daughter so desperately needed. We must take control of our emotions, get out of our feelings, be made whole.

PRAYER:

Dear Father,

As I seek to find my place of peace in every area of my life, I call on Jehovah Shalom the God of my peace to help me get out of my feelings and get my emotions in check. In Jesus Name. Amen.

SCRIPTURE FOCUS: Matthew 15:25-27

"Then came she and worshipped him, saying, Lord, help me. But he answered and said, "It is not meet to take the children's bread, and to cast it to dogs. And she said, Truth, Lord: yet the dogs eat of the crumbs which fall from their master's table"

AFFIRMING FOCUS:

Get out Your Feelings! You have work to do. Whatever happened or is happening, didn't come to kill you, it came to build you. Remember... ***"One bad moment does not make bad day." ~Desiree G. Briggs***

MY SPACE FOR REFLECTING

(IT IS WRITTEN)

DAY ELEVEN

TAME THAT THING!

The Bible declares in ***James 3:7-8, "For every kind of beasts, and of birds, and of things in the sea, is tamed, and hath been tamed by mankind: But the tongue can no man tame; it is an unruly evil, full of deadly poison."*** Unruly, evil, full of deadly poison; no it's not a snake, it's the tongue. From whence bitter and sweet flow from. How can this be? Can a fountain spring forth bitter and sweet water? Fresh water and salt? Yet, that is the condition of the tongue. The same tongue we will bless one person, and from that same tongue, curse someone else out. We say sweet nothings from that tongue and express sentiments of undying love, and from the same tongue, we've turned around and lied to that same person. Releases words that pierce the heart and soul. It is easier to tame a snake than the tongue in our mouths. Why is that? Glad you asked. The Bible says that from the abundance of heart the mouth (tongue)speaks. The tongue releases, and flows the issues of life, that are housed in the heart of man. Often times it is our unresolved issues that enables us to be cool, calm, and collective one moment, then flip out on someone the next. The tongue releases the venom of pinned up frustrations, life altering experiences, suppressed emotions, and the everyday cares of life. When we fail to cast our cares upon Him who cares for us; then that untamable, unruly, venomous tongue can literally kill someone. There are plenty of victims dead and alive that have been the target of a tongue that had no rule over it; That child who's been bullied to the point of no return, by their peers who had no understanding of the trigger they pulled, with their tongue. The verbally abusive wife, who's torn down the self esteem of her husband, and now he seeks comfort and peace in the arms of another woman. **Proverbs 25:24** says, ***"It is better to dwell on the rooftop, than inside the house with a nagging woman."*** A woman who can't control her tongue. Ask God to help you tame your tongue, it could cost you your home.

PRAYER:

Dear Father,

I confess, I am guilty of being both bitter and sweet. Releasing both freshwater and salt. As I read the words in this chapter, I saw myself. I seek to tame my tongue in Your word. Speaking the language of the Kingdom, releasing all experiences that would cause me to release venom that could hurt, destroy, and or kill someone else. Thank You Lord for taming my tongue. In Jesus Name. Amen.

SCRIPTURE FOCUS: James 3:7-8,

"For every kind of beasts, and of birds, and of things in the sea, is tamed, and hath been tamed by mankind: But the tongue can no man tame; it is an unruly evil, full of deadly poison."

AFFIRMING FOCUS:

Today I vow to make a conscious decision to guard my tongue. To be mindful of the words I release from my mouth. May they be life and light only. My tongue is being tamed.

MY SPACE FOR REFLECTING

(IT IS WRITTEN)

DAY TWELVE

NO DEPOSIT NO WITHDRAWAL

Do you know if you showed up to a bank and passed a withdrawal slip to a teller at an institution where you don't have an account, demanding money, you could be charged with armed robbery? Why, because you can't make a withdrawal request where you don't have an account, and you haven't made a deposit. This is true in a lot of scenarios in life. You can't withdraw love where you haven't deposited love. You can't withdraw support where you haven't supported. You can't expect from others what they can't expect from you. You see, the law of sowing and reaping is parallel to deposit and withdrawal. You can't get out what you don't put in. Many times in life it may seem like you are the only one making all the deposits, doing all the sowing. Remember, where you sow, and make deposits, is just as important as what you sow and where you deposit. If you sow in bad ground, or deposit in an institution with no FDIC protection, you run the risk of lost, no return, nothing to withdraw. We must be mindful and intentional about where we sow and make deposits. When it comes to harvesting, we must make sure that we are sowing and depositing what we want to receive, the return that we want to see. There is nothing worse than getting a harvest of something you didn't want. Yet, that's the return of the deposit or the seeds you sowed. Often in relationships whether intimate or platonic, we tend to be overly invested. By nature we are nurturers; we tend to give, invest, deposit, and sow, where there is no reciprocation. This is not necessarily a bad thing, but it is important that you inspect the soil before you start sowing seeds. What's the track record of the individual? Do their relationships normally last for any significant amount of time? Are they sowers/ investors? It's important that you research the integrity and strength of the institution before you make a deposit. What's the yield? What's the APR? Remember, no deposit, no withdrawal!

PRAYER:

Dear Father,

I am guilty of desiring to reap where I haven't sown. Looking to withdraw from where I didn't deposit. I understand that sowing and reaping, deposit and withdrawal is a law, which yields a return of its kind. I will sow what I desire to grow. In Jesus Name. Amen.

SCRIPTURE FOCUS: Galatians 6:7

"Be not deceived; God is not mocked: for whatsoever a man soweth, that shall he also reap."

AFFIRMING FOCUS:

Seed sown is harvest grown. I will sow good seeds. Make deposits where there are needs. So, that in my time of harvest I will reap what I've sown; and in my time of need, deposits can be withdrawn.

MY SPACE FOR REFLECTING

(IT IS WRITTEN)

DAY THIRTEEN

CONSEQUENCES OF YOUR CHOICE

The awesome thing about the world we live in is that God our Father, and creator, gave us the freedom to choose. From the very foundation of the world, a choice was made by Adam and Eve, that had a consequence that impacted the world. Enticed by the serpent, they made a choice to eat of the tree which God told them not to eat of. They made a choice. The responsibility and consequences of that choice has had a rippling affect throughout eternity. While evil was created for God's glory, to choose evil over good is a choice. Right over wrong, a choice. You not only have the right to choose, you have to be willing to accept the impact, whether good or bad, of your choice. We have all made decisions, choices we regret. Choices we didn't think all the way through. Some of those choices have had devastating impacts. What do you think would happen, if before we made a choice, a decision, we seek the wisdom and counsel of God? I'll tell you what would happen. We'd avoid some of the pitfalls, dead ends, and roadblocks we find ourselves faced with in life. Yes, the freedom has been given to man by God, yet we don't always make right decisions. I believe that mistakes are necessary, and they provide a place from which we can grow, this is also a choice. We choose to learn and grow from our mistakes or we repeat them because we choose not to. How will you exercise your right to choose; your freedom of choice? When we choose not to settle for a man, just to say we have a man, we made the choice to embrace our value, our worth. When we choose to eat a salad over a burger, or take the stairs over the elevator, we made the choice to invest in our health. There is a choice we will all have to make, and that's the choice to live, so that we live again. When we accept and receive Jesus Christ as our Lord and Savior, we've made the choice to live, to live again. You have a right to choose. Choose wisely and live, it is your choice!

PRAYER:

Dear Father,

I want to thank You for giving me the freedom of choice. The ability to choose regardless of the outcome, it is my choice. Today I make the choice to live in Your Will, according to Your Statuses. In Jesus Name. Amen.

SCRIPTURE FOCUS: Deuteronomy 30:19 "I call heaven and earth to record this day against you, that I have set before you life and death, blessings and cursing: therefore choose life, that both thou and thy seed my live:"

AFFIRMING FOCUS:

The choice to live my life the way I want to is mine. I can choose to live it like Mary J and say, **"My Life Is Fine."** However, I choose not to. I submit my life, my will, and my way to the Father on today. It's my choice.

MY SPACE FOR REFLECTING

(IT IS WRITTEN)

DAY FOURTEEN

A DEFINING MOMENT!

The definition of a thing can change its entire meaning. So can the interpretation of the receiver. Which is why it is so important to make sure that all communications, whether tangible or verbal, are understood by both parties. The worst thing that can take place in an act of kindness, is the misinterpretation thereof. Which is why it is so important for all parties involved, to have a clear understanding of what is being communicated. For instance, someone you are crushing on is always telling you they love you in passing, but they mean it in a platonic/friendship way. Meanwhile, based on your definition of the word love for this individual, because you're crushing on them in a romantic, relationship way, you've reserved the church, picked the colors, and picked the wedding party. I know it may seems extreme, farfetched, it hits closer to home than you think. Yet, for reason's like this it is so important to make

sure you have clear and defined understandings of communications, of all forms, because communication isn't just verbal. Some actions speak louder than any conversation could ever communicate. For instance, the Bible says, in ***John 3:16 "For God so loved the world, that He gave His***

only begotten Son, that whosoever believeth in him should not perish, but have everlasting life." This is clearly the ultimate act/action of love. God communicated His love for us not just through lip service, but the ultimate action of sacrifice. Yet, as sacrificial as the death of Jesus Christ is, there are still those that won't receive it. Those that can't understand or comprehend it. Does their lack of understanding change the defining act? No, of course not, but sadly, because their definition or interpretation of it reads different, they reject the love. They've chosen other gods, idols. We are so special to God that not only did He define His love for us in John 3:16, He demonstrated it on the cross at Calvary. Don't go through life trying to interpret what someone means, just simply ask, "Can you define that please?"

PRAYER:

Dear Father,

I know I have made a lot of bad choices and decisions based on my understanding or definition of a thing. Many misunderstandings I've experienced as a result of the lack of definition. Today, I seek, wisdom and understanding, so that there are no more misunderstandings. In Jesus Name. Amen.

SCRIPTURE FOCUS: Proverbs 4:7

"Wisdom is the principal thing; therefore get wisdom: and with all thy getting get understanding."

AFFIRMING FOCUS:

I will say what I mean and be clear when I say it. I won't leave it up for interpretation. A clear understanding of what someone is saying, can make all the difference. A defining moment.

MY SPACE FOR REFLECTING

(IT IS WRITTEN)

DAY FIFTEEN

WHAT'S IN YOUR FRUIT SALAD?

Fruit without root is plastic fruit. Do you remember going to your grandma's house and on the dining room table was a bowl of fruit, only this fruit was plastic. It was there for decoration not for consumption. I remember the first time I discovered plastic fruit. I went to grandma's house and there they were, the big beautiful green grapes. My mouth was ready. I grabbed them. Only to discover they were plastic, not meant for eating. I was so disappointed because I was hungry. All the fruit in the bowl on the table looked real, but they were all plastic. Plastic fruit. Jesus had a similar experience in ***Mark 11:13*** when He and His disciples were traveling from Bethany. He was hungry and saw a fig tree afar off. When He had come upon it, there was only leaves, for the time of the figs had not yet come. The tree had evidence of fruit, there were leaves; yet, there was no fruit for consumption found. Have you ever perceived something from the outside, only to discover once you got close enough to it, it wasn't what you thought it was? They weren't who you thought they were? You weren't who you thought you were? Many say that they are Christians. To be a Christian is to be Christ like. To have the character and integrity, and Spirit of Christ. Yet, many of those same people lack fruit that remain. Fruit that's sustained. What fruit is that? Glad you asked. It is fruit with root. That's the fruit of the Spirit, of Christ. There are nine fruit of the Spirit; love, joy, peace, longsuffering, gentleness, goodness, faith, Meekness, temperance: against such there is no law. The nine make up the Spirit, which defines the character of Christ. If you have love, joy, peace, but you lack longsuffering, you have a spirit, but it's not The Spirit of Jesus Christ. Your fruit salad must contain love, joy, peace, gentleness, goodness, faith, Meekness, and temperance. The combination of the nine don't mean you'll be sweet all of the time, what it does provide is root for your fruit, that will remain.

PRAYER:

Dear Father,

I desire fruit that remain. Fruit with root. I want to be more like Christ. I declare and decree the nine fruit of the Spirit lives in and through me. Love, joy, peace, longsuffering, gentleness, goodness, faith, Meekness, temperance. In Jesus Name. Amen.

SCRIPTURE FOCUS: Galatians 5:22
"But the fruit of the Spirit is love, joy, peace, longsuffering, gentleness, goodness, faith, Meekness, temperance: against such there is no law."

AFFIRMING FOCUS:

Plastic fruit don't have root! I'm grounded and rooted in Christ, my fruit will remain. My fruit salad consist of love, joy, peace, longsuffering, gentleness, goodness, faith, Meekness, and temperance, I have all nine!

MY SPACE FOR REFLECTING

(IT IS WRITTEN)

DAY SIXTEEN

GO TELL THAT

In a world where everything is on blast! Everything is tell! Tell! It's caught on camera, and did for the VINE (LOL)! Nothing is secret or scared. We tell this, and we tell that. Social media has become the platform of gossip. Don't get me wrong, it's not all negative, discouraging, belittling, demeaning, the latest millrun scandalous topics. No not all, but most. Our timelines are flooded with it. I'm not sure we understand the impact of what we communicate. One racial or bias post can incite a whole riot. Comments full of venom, the kind laced with hatred. What do you think would be the impact if we intentionally started spreading the goodness of Jesus Christ. The blessings that He's bestowed upon our lives. Telling of His goodness. The miracles we've experienced in our lives more than rumors, lies, and gossip? We actually have a responsibility to share our testimonies, not for our glory, but for the Glory of God. The Bible declares in **Revelation 12:11a "And they overcame him (Satan) by the blood of the Lamb, and by the word of their testimony;"** Which simply says, if God brought us through it; He healed our body; saved our soul and that of our family; if He provided in the wilderness, in the midst of a pandemic; if He kept the death angel from visiting our house; if He put food on the table; if He kept our mind when the enemy was trying to take it; if He didn't allow the sickness or the diseases of Egypt to come upon us; if He didn't allow our son or daughter to be mishandled by the police, killed in gang violence, or be the victim of a violent crime; if He gave you the job you prayed for, knowing you weren't qualified for; if He made sure that all your bills were paid; made sure the doctor gave you a good report; if He kept you thriving in the midst of others losing their jobs; Then go tell that! By doing so, you overcome, you shine the light and love of Christ and bring hope to others. Now that's something to talk about!

PRAYER:

Dear Father,

I'll tell it! I'll tell it! I'll tell of your goodness and all that You have done for me. You never cease to amaze or provide for me. For that I'm grateful and I'm going to tell it everywhere I go. Get Your Glory Lord! In Jesus Name. Amen.

SCRIPTURE FOCUS: Revelation 12:11a

"And they overcame him by the blood of the Lamb, and by the word of their testimony;"

AFFIRMING FOCUS:

I'll tell it! I'll tell it, everywhere I go. God's been too good to me, for me not to tell you so. Through all my good times and my bad. Through my happy times and my sad. God's been good! I'll tell it!

MY SPACE FOR REFLECTING

(IT IS WRITTEN)

DAY SEVENTEEN

THE SILENT KILLER

To forgive or not to forgive, that's a struggle most people have when hurt or betrayed. Some struggle because of the depth of the offense, the betrayal, and some struggle because of pride. Unforgiveness is a silent killer. It slowly eats away at the very fabric of the individual holding on to it. Your joy is impacted, there cease to be peace, and your relationships are strained; because of one bad experience you treat everyone the same. Is it them, or is it really you to blame? Wait a minute allow me to explain, you see, they may be the ones to blame for the offense and for your initial pain, but how long will you allow the experience to control you and have that kind of power over you. The impact of unforgiveness can cause years of delay, your quality of life to decay. What I hope you learn and take away from this reading today, is the silent killer of unforgiveness only has the power you give it. I challenge you to make up in your mind that today is the last day you will nurse the pain of yesterday. Today you will forgive and release the person(s) that hurt you; the person(s) that lied to you, lied on you; today you will take the first step to be free. Free from the prison unforgiveness has locked you in. The greatest example of forgiveness is found in ***Luke 23:33-34***

"And when they were come to the place, which is called Calvary, where they crucified him, and the malefactors, one on the right hand, and the other on the left. Then said Jesus, Father forgive them; for they know not what they do." Here we have the greatest example of all times. He was without sin, He'd done no wrong, yet they saw fit to crucify Him without a cause, but before He took His last breath, He did what I consider a very selfless act, He asked God to forgive those that were responsible for His crucifixion, His death. In the Our Father's prayer found in Matthew 6:12 we must ask God to forgive our debts, trespasses, as we forgive those who are indebted to us, who trespass against us. Forgive, it's not easy but don't allow the silent killer to silently kill you.

PRAYER:

Dear Father,

I will not allow the silent assassin of unforgiveness to kill me. I pray for deliverance from past hurts and offenses. Those that were done to me and those that I have done. Forgive me my debts as I forgive my debtors. In Jesus Name. Amen.

SCRIPTURE FOCUS: Matthew 6:12

"And forgive us our debts, as we forgive our debtors."

AFFIRMING FOCUS:

I acknowledge I've been here too long, a place of bitterness and unforgiveness. I release those that have hurt me and those through whom offense has come. I give myself permission to forgive and live!

MY SPACE FOR REFLECTING

(IT IS WRITTEN)

DAY EIGHTTEEN

AN APPOINTED TIME

Today as I sit wondering, I stare out my window and I think to myself, when will my time ever come. It seems as if I've been waiting forever, and forever I still wait. Waiting for the manifestation of my promise. The promise I received from God concerning my life. The promise of abundant success, love, joy, and peace. Will it come to past, will it ever happen for me? I cried and prayed; I prayed and cried; for the possibility of the promise, my hope has died. I'm getting tired of waiting, as I watch others get blessed. She *ain't* even trying to live right, and she's picking out her wedding dress! She's getting married! I can't even get a date! Something's wrong with this picture. How long must I wait? I'm waiting for God to answer; say something, give me a sign please! Time is passing by. Will it ever happen for me? "Your time is coming!" If I hear that one more time! My time is now! Now I want what's mine! Patience is a virtue, this may be true, but my patience is wearing thin, I need God to come through. When will it be my turn? When will my time come? That's it! I'm tired of waiting! I'm going after it! Promise here I come! The Bible declares in **Habakkuk 2:3 "For the vision is yet for an appointed time, but at the end it shall speak, and not lie; though it tarry, wait for it; because**

it will surely come, it will not tarry." I know it's hard to stand by and watch as others are seemingly winning, thriving, and passing you; just remember, their vision had an appointed time too. So, just because she got married before you, started her business before you, had a baby before you, wrote the book before you, it doesn't mean that you won't accomplish the things that are in your heart too; the things God has promised to bring to past for you. You must keep the faith, hold on and be strong. As you see her win, congratulate her, because they'll be a time when she'll congratulate you too. Wait on the Lord, your appointed time draws near. God made you a promise and let's get one thing clear, He cannot lie.

PRAYER:

Dear Father,

I know that patience isn't one of my strong traits. Waiting has become hard, but I trust Your timing, I trust you God. Give me the patience that is required to wait on You, as I wait for my appointed time. In Jesus Name. Amen.

SCRIPTURE FOCUS: Habakkuk 2:3

"For the vision is yet for an appointed time, but at the end it shall speak, and not lie; though it tarry, wait for it; because it will surely come, it will not tarry."

AFFIRMING FOCUS:

Waiting might not be the easiest thing to do, but if you learn to wait on God, He'll always come through. He's an on-time God, and there's an appointed time for you. Wait on the Lord.

MY SPACE FOR REFLECTING

(IT IS WRITTEN)

DAY NINETEEN

FAITH IT, DON'T FAKE IT!

There's a saying that says, "Fake it till you make it!" and that is literally what most have done all their life. Faking and or pretending to do, be, or have something they do not. The issue with faking it until you make it, is that most people stay in the fake zone so long, they begin to believe their own lie. The Bible tells us that the just shall live by faith. This is found in **Romans 1:17**. The righteousness of God is revealed from faith to faith. To fake and or pretend about anything can be draining, because ultimately, the lie, the mirage, that has been manufactured, eventually has to be proven, produced, or justified. How long can one go on pretending to be married to someone who doesn't even know the two of you are in a relationship? How long before it's revealed you weren't telling the truth about the house you are renting, but telling everyone you brought it, is discovered? How long can you get away with having a form of Godliness and no power? How long? You see what I mean, it's exhausting just writing about it. People put on for the Vine, and the Gram every day, all day. Don't get caught up in that. When we choose to truly live by faith, we cause God to not only move on our behalf, but to bring forth the manifestation of the thing we are believing Him for. Faith is putting your trust in the character of who God is. The God that will not and cannot lie. We don't have to fake it when we know who our source is. Abba Father has given us the authority to walk by faith and not by sight. To not give in to the pressures of life to be like someone else. If you don't have the body you desire, you just have to have the discipline, trainer, and nutritionist for it. The faith to believe that you can achieve anything you put your mind to. The pressure to keep up with the Jones' will have you living a lie, faking the funk. On the other hand, to possess the things you desire in life, requires faith and works. Have faith, do the work, then whatsoever you desire shall be.

PRAYER:

Dear Father,

I trust Your will and plan for my life. I will be anxious for nothing. I have faith for my journey, for my process. Thank You for Your faithfulness towards me. I shall continue to live by faith.

In Jesus Name. Amen.

SCRIPTURE FOCUS: Romans 1:17

"For therein is the righteousness of God revealed from faith to faith: as it is written, The just shall live by faith."

AFFIRMING FOCUS:

Faith is trust. Faith is the belief or conviction of the truth of anything. Faith is assurance. Faith is also the character of one who can be relied upon. God, I have faith in You! No faking it for me.

MY SPACE FOR REFLECTING

(IT IS WRITTEN)

DAY TWENTY

LORD FLOW THROUGH ME

When a seed is planted in the ground, watered and nurtured, it begins to develop, and establish roots. The manifestation of what is taking place beneath the earth will eventually produce what will be seen above the earth. This is the fruit of the seed. Every seed produces of its kind. If you plant apple seeds, it will produce an apple tree. If you plant rose seeds, it will produce a rose bush. The law of sowing and reaping is relevant here. You can't sow orange seeds expecting peaches. For whatsoever a man soweth that shall he also reap. With that understanding in mind, the scripture tells us in ***2 Corinthians 9:10, "Now he that ministereth seed to the sower both minister bread for your food, and multiply your seed sown, and increase the fruits of your righteousness;"*** God gives seed to the **SOWER!** When we purpose in our hearts to be a vessel God can flow the wealth of the Kingdom through, the Bible declares He gives us the seed to sow. You see, there is no bank in heaven. There is no check coming to your house signed God. God uses people; and if God can get it through you He's going to give it to you. You are the fertile ground God wants to flow the wealth of the Kingdom through. Sowing is a lifestyle. When you purpose in your heart to be a **RIVER**, a Kingdom financial institution in the earth, that God can trust. He's going to make sure that you have seed to sow; seed for every good work; seed for what your family needs; and seed for the ministry/vision in your heart. You won't have to take from one, to sustain the other. God gives seed to the sower for sowing. As a sower, you aren't just given financial seeds to sow, you are also empowered to sow seeds of love, reflective of the love of Jesus Christ. There will be many opportunities for you to allow the love of Christ to flow through you. This is expressed in different ways; a hug; a smile; an act of kindness; a word spoken in season. As a RIVER, a vessel that God can trust let Him flow through you!

PRAYER:

Dear Father,

You can trust me. I submit myself to be used by You. I am a Sower. Lord, thank You for seed to sow. Thank You for flowing the wealth of the Kingdom through me. In Jesus Name. Amen.

SCRIPTURE FOCUS: 2 Corinthians 9:10, "Now he that ministereth seed to the sower both minister bread for your food, and multiply your seed sown, and increase the fruits of your righteousness;"

AFFIRMING FOCUS:

Flow like a RIVER Lord. Flow like a river Lord in me, Lord flow through me. I'm an extension of Your hands, I wanna be kind to my fellow man; for this is the Kingdom's plan. I wanna bless everyone I see, Lord I'm a RIVER You can trust me. You can flow through me. Give it to me.

MY SPACE FOR REFLECTING

(IT IS WRITTEN)

DAY TWENTY-ONE

HOPE AGAISNT HOPE

Has God made you a promise and due to your own limited ability, you thought it impossible to come to past? You know like the one He made Abraham , who was Seventy-Five years old, and his wife Sara was Sixty-five, when they received the promise that Abraham, who had no children of his own, would be the father of many nations. Many years had passed by since God had made him the promise, and still no heir. No name sake. How would he become the father of many nations when he didn't have a son? Sara and Abraham were getting older. Sara figured she would help God out, and gave him permission to go to her handmaiden who would conceive and bare Abraham a child. God told Abraham that He would make him the father of many nations. He didn't need Sara's help. He just required Abraham's faith. Even though it was twenty-five years later, Abraham and Sara received the child that would bring God's promise He made Abraham to past. Isaac was the promise. Though Abraham was 100 years old and Sara was 90, the promise came to past. Abraham had to hope against hope. When what would seem impossible with man, was then, now, and shall always be possible with God. I know in the current climate in which we live, it's hard to hope against hope when all seems hopeless. Yet, God has made you a promise, and not one word He's spoken concerning your life shall fall to the ground. No, not one. Your vision, promise shall come to past. Your vision will speak and not lie. Even if it takes twenty-five years for it to manifest in your life, fret not, fear not, nor be dismayed, for what the Lord has begun in your life, He shall complete it unto the day of Jesus Christ. So, hope against hope, you have the winning odds. Just be steadfast and unmovable. Keep the faith, Abraham did. He knew his ability to father a child would be something only God could do. So, Keep hope alive in your heart!

PRAYER:

Dear Father,

All my hope is in You. All my hope is in You. I trust Your every word concerning my life and everything connected to me. All my hope is in You God. You're the light of the world. In Jesus Name. Amen.

SCRIPTURE FOCUS: Romans: 4:18

"Who against hope believed in hope, that he might become the father of many nations, according to that which was spoken. So shall thy seed be."

AFFIRMING FOCUS:

Blessed is the man who's hope the Lord is. Lord you are my hope, and because you are my hope I am blessed, better than blessed. Thank You Lord.

MY SPACE FOR REFLECTING

(IT IS WRITTEN)

DAY TWENTY TWO

HERE WE ARE, MAKING IT!

The loss of anything, a love one, a family member, a job, a relationship, a marriage, can take a toll on our minds, bodies and spirits. No one ever wants to experience any type of loss, but loss of any kind is inevitable as we travel through this thing called life. The whys and what ifs of situations can sometimes keep our minds stuck in bad places. Many people have never imagined themselves on the bad side of the equation of divorce, unemployed, homeless, or grieving a death. As real as these tragedies have happened in our lives, we must know that there is a real God who is a mind regulator and restorer of all things. No, we cannot bring people back from the dead, although I wish we could. He has assured us that He is a giver of peace, even in death. Peace that surpasses all understanding **(Philippians 4:7).** Feelings that are associated with loss should be expressed, but we must remember that they are just the way we feel at that moment. There is hope that our feelings will change to something positive in the future. So, sis, let the tears flow. We are humans. After it is all said and done, we must turn back to our heavenly father for strength, courage, and comfort. It is only when we get to the other side of a thing that we can look back and say, "I made it!" Every day through the process, we can say, "here I am, making it!" There is no right or wrong way to process loss. We must deal with situations knowing we are not alone naturally or spiritually. The enemy wants us to isolate ourselves from the world, but we must rally around those who naturally love and care about us when we are dealing with loss or grief, so we can make it!

PRAYER:

Dear Father

As I have experienced many losses in my time, thank you for the gains that I have made. Here I am making it because of your unconditional love for me. I see your hand in every situation, even the bad and traumatic experiences. Thank you, Jesus! Because of your unwavering love, I can look back and say, "I made it! In Jesus Name. Amen.

SCRIPTURE FOCUS: II Corinthians 1:3-4 "Praise be to the God and Father of our Lord Jesus Christ, the Father of compassion and the God of all comfort, who comforts us in all our troubles, so that we can comfort those in any trouble with the comfort we ourselves receive from God."

AFFIRMING FOCUS:

I have great joy knowing that even through my loss, I have gained! Every day the Father wakes me up is a joyous day to realize that I'm still here making it!

MY SPACE FOR REFLECTING

(IT IS WRITTEN)

DAY TWENTY-THREE

IT COULD BE WORSE

We sometimes think, when our backs are against the wall, when there has been a domino effect of bad things to occur in our lives, what else could go wrong? We have to be careful what we ask for. Bad situations and circumstances can put our minds in a terrible place to think we are alone and no one cares about us. Ask yourself this, "What is it that my heavenly father wants me to learn from all of this?" God's servant Job was stripped of everything remotely possible in his life, but it could have been worse. Although Job lost it all, his life was spared. When are facing adversity, it seems almost impossible to see ourselves on the other side of the adversity. Contrary to what our adversary, the devil, wants us to think, our lives have been spared. The Bible reminds us to think on things that are true, right, noble, pure and lovely. **(Philippians 4:8),** even in uncertain times, think on these things. Our thinking plays a major part in how we see our situations. Every day we are blessed to open our eyes, is another opportunity to see things differently then what we see with our natural eyes. As sure as we live, there will certainly be mountain top and valley experiences. Some experiences will make us feel like we have gained the whole world, and some experiences will have us feeling like we have lost it all. God wants to make sure that His children know they can always lean on Him during difficult times. Believing in Him doesn't eliminate our problems, it does reassure us we never have to face them alone ever again. So instead of asking yourself "what else could go wrong?", be thankful because it could be much worse.

PRAYER:

Dear Father,

Thank you for sparing my life in times of adversity. I realize that you have never left me, nor forsaken me. Thank you for your continuous grace that covers me when I can't see past my own situations. I trust you to carry me through. In Jesus Name. Amen.

SCRIPTURE FOCUS: I Peter 5:10

"And to the God of all grace, who called you to His eternal Glory in Christ, after you have suffered a little while, will himself restore you and make you strong, firm and steadfast."

AFFIRMING FOCUS:

I will no longer ask what more could happen? I will see God's hand in everything, even when it does not seem like He is there. I know He is working it all out for my good.

MY SPACE FOR REFLECTING

(IT IS WRITTEN)

DAY TWENTY-FOUR

WHAT LEGACY ARE YOU LEAVING BEHIND?

We often think that legacy is leaving behind something once a person has passed away. We often associate it with something monetary or materialistic when we talk about legacy. Legacy is much more than something monetary or materialistic when someone has died. It is more about sharing what you have learned not just what you have earned. Material wealth is just a small portion of legacy. A person that leaves someone a lot of money after they have died without the wisdom of how to maintain the wealth, is only setting the person up for failure. Legacy involves intentional and strategic planning. Positioning the next generation for success. Our legacy will outlive us. God's legacy for us, goes far beyond anything materialistic or monetary. His greatest commandment was that we love our neighbors as ourselves. As we live to leave a legacy for those who will come behind us, our greatest example should be acts of kindness and compassion to our fellow brothers and sisters. Jesus showed us through His obedience to the father, that we could achieve this because he passed the legacy on to us. Our focus should not only be to leave money for our loved one, but we should leave a legacy that continuously glorifies the father. Humility, obedience, and faithfulness are just a few attributes we can leave as we live godly lives that can be passed down for many generations to come. Don't forget the legacy of love. It is currently what the world could surely use more of. What legacy are you leaving behind?

PRAYER:

Dear Father,

I seek your wisdom and ask that you lead me and make clear to me the legacy I am to leave behind. Thank you Lord, for the legacy and example set before me through your only son Jesus. Help me to follow His example and leave a legacy that will be passed down to future generations to come. In Jesus Name. Amen.

SCRIPTURE FOCUS: Psalms 112:2-3

"Their children will be mighty in the land; the generation of the upright will be blessed. Wealth and riches are in their houses, and their righteousness endures forever."

AFFIRMING FOCUS:

I will leave an unselfish legacy that my heavenly father will be proud of. A legacy of not only riches, but of love, wisdom and knowledge that can continuously be passed down.

MY SPACE FOR REFLECTING

(IT IS WRITTEN)

DAY TWENTY-FIVE

WHAT SAYETH YOU ABOUT YOU?

Tell me something sister, why is it that we have a hard time believing all the wonderful things that our Creator has to say about us? His word confirms over and over how much He loves us and how much we should love ourselves. Have you ever looked in the mirror and didn't like what you saw? What was it about the woman in the mirror that made you come to that conclusion? Was her body shaped funny? Were her lips too full or too thin? Perhaps you thought her nose was too large, too thin or crooked. All of these external qualities have nothing to do with the internal makeup of who we were created to be. His word reminds us that the Lord does not look at the things man looks at. Man looks at the outward appearance, but the Lord looks at the heart **(I Samuel 16:7)**. In order to get past our external flaws, we must dig deep into our internal makeup. To fully understand that, we should know that we are fearfully and wonderfully made, just as His word declares **(Psalm 139:14)**. Our heavenly father loves us unconditionally. He accepts our external and internal flaws! He sees us as loved, forgiven, beautiful, and exquisite in His eyes.

Negative actions and words have chipped away at the very thought that a perfect God could love such and imperfect being like us. Once we accept and start to speak His word over our lives, we can push past the negativity and live a more fulfilled life, both internally and externally. Now look at the amazing person in the mirror! Look past her external flaws and see the beautiful creature that is fearfully and wonderfully made because that's WHAT I SAY ABOUT ME! What say you about you?

PRAYER:

Dear Father,

Thank You that I am Your daughter and Your beautiful creation. Forgive me for seeing and thinking of myself to be anything less than how You see me. Continue to show me the amazing things about myself that I have not yet noticed.

In Jesus Name. Amen.

SCRIPTURE FOCUS: Song of Solomon 4:7 "You are altogether beautiful, my darling; there is no flaw in you."

AFFIRMING FOCUS:

I am beautiful. I am loved. I am fearfully and wonderfully made. Jesus loves me just the way I am, flaws and all.

MY SPACE FOR REFLECTING

(IT IS WRITTEN)

DAY TWENTY-SIX

JUST DO IT, ALREADY!

We've all heard the phrase, delayed, but not denied. That usually refers to waiting for blessings or prayers to be answered from God. Many times, that phrase is used because we want the blessings and the prayers to be answered, but usually struggle with putting in the work that is required to achieve the desired results. Many opportunities await us throughout this lifetime, but we tend to procrastinate on moving forward in them. We have become a pro at putting things off until a later date, and then we are pressured to complete the task at the last minute. Many will claim that they work well under pressure, but that may just be another excuse as to why they haven't achieved the goal or task sooner than the deadline. Many procrastinate because of fear, doubt, wanting everything to be perfect, or simply refuse to change. Either way, this bad habit is not of God. Putting things off until a later time is not honoring the gift of time that God has given us. He is expecting us to be fruitful with our time, and when we don't, there are usually consequences that we do not want to answer to. If we spend too much time deliberating about what to do, we usually loose the motivation to do it. Diligence, consistency, and perseverance are ways to overcome this terrible spirit of procrastination that has robbed us of opportunities. We should give ourselves measurable deadlines to complete even the simplest tasks if we struggle with procrastination. Remember that baby steps are still steps. Jesus could return at any moment, and we do not want Him to find us with our work undone.

PRAYER:

Dear Father,

Forgive me for putting things off and using excuses as to why I could not complete an assignment. I now realize that I was not honoring you with my time. I pray that you would redeem any time that I may have lost. Thank you for deliverance of this spirit of procrastination. In Jesus Name. Amen.

SCRIPTURE FOCUS: Proverbs 12:24
"Diligent hands will rule, but laziness ends in forced labor."

AFFIRMING FOCUS:

I will honor God with my time by not procrastinating with tasks and assignments. I will NOT put off for later, what can be achieved now. I will just do it already!

MY SPACE FOR REFLECTING

(IT IS WRITTEN)

DAY TWENTY-SEVEN

FOR THE LOVE OF MONEY

Money can add unwanted anxiety to our lives, but we have been called to steward His riches here on Earth. That means, everything He allows us to possess, He wants us to manage well. First of all, we have to understand that money is just the resource, a tool in this economic society. God is our source. The bible declares that the Earth is the Lord's and the fullness there of, the world and all who live in it **(Psalm 24:1)**. Therefore we know that all the money belongs to God. The economic system is set up so we will forever be enslaved to the lender, but God says, ***"The rich rule over the poor, and the borrower is slave to the lender." (Psalm 22:7***). We must position ourselves to no longer be slaves to our own finances. The first principle to repositioning our finances is honoring Him in tithes and monetary offerings. God does not want or need our money, He wants our heart. This giving is a leap of faith and an act of obedience to His word. We are saying, Lord, I trust you to be the provider in my life for my family in every situation. He also wants us to save and eliminate our debt. We are the directors of where our money goes. We tell it what to do and where to go, instead of it being the other way around.

The enemy is sowing seeds of greed across the land, but it is up to us to kill that spirit, transform our minds, and renew our way of thinking when it comes to our finances. Pray for His wisdom as you move forward in you newness of faith through your finances.

PRAYER:

Dear Father,

I humbly submit all my finances over to you. I pray that you will guide me on how to be a better steward of my finances so I can provide for my family. I trust you, Lord. You have never failed me. Thank you for this fresh wind of wisdom when it comes to my finances. In Jesus Name. Amen.

SCRIPTURE FOCUS: I Timothy 6:10

"For the love of money is a root of all kinds of evil. Some people, eager for money, have wandered from the faith and pierced themselves with many grief's."

AFFIRMING FOCUS:

I will no longer be a slave to my own finances. I trust God's infinite wisdom when it comes to my finances. I am rich in wisdom and in wealth.

MY SPACE FOR REFLECTING

(IT IS WRITTEN)

DAY TWENTY-EIGHT

I LOVE ME SOME ME!

As women, we slowly place ourselves at the end of our own chain. We seem to be last on the list when it comes to taking care of ourselves. When we think of "self-care," we sometimes think we are being selfish if we take care of ourselves first. Truthfully, if we don't put ourselves back to the top of our own list, we will not be fit to take care of those we love, and those who depend on us. Self-care doesn't always have to involve spending money or carving large chunks of time out of our already busy day. A longer than usual uninterrupted bath, an extra 5 minutes in the shower, journaling, listening to your favorite song two to three times in a row, are just a few, of many ways to enhance our moods. Spiritually speaking, God wants the best version of us. ***Romans 12:1*** states, ***"Therefore, I urge you, brothers and sisters, in view of God's mercy, to offer your bodies as a living sacrifice, holy and pleasing to God—this is your true and proper worship."*** Taking care of ourselves is a form of worship to the father. When we offer ourselves as a living sacrifice, we are giving God the best version of ourselves. The enemy will try to guilt us into thinking taking time for ourselves is unnecessary, but we should slow down and take inventory of ourselves in order to know how we can replenish our minds, bodies, and spirits, to be more effective as we continue this journey. It's necessary to be refreshed so we can be prepared for what lies ahead. Sister, we can't be everything to everyone, and we can't do it all for everybody. The word "NO" is a sentence all by itself. ~Selah

PRAYER:

Dear Father,

Thank you for this precious gift called life. I offer my life back to you as a living sacrifice. Thank you for the strength and the boldness to take care of myself first. In Jesus Name. Amen.

SCRIPTURE FOCUS: I Corinthians 6:19-20 "Do you not know that your bodies are temples of the Holy Spirit, who is in you, whom you have received from God? You are not your own; you were bought at a price. Therefore, honor God with your bodies."

AFFIRMING FOCUS:

I will take better care of my mind. I will take better care of my body. I will take better care of my spirit, for it all belongs to the Lord.

MY SPACE FOR REFLECTING

(IT IS WRITTEN)

DAY TWENTY-NINE

LOVE AND CHERISH

We often let the word "love" roll off of our tongues with such ease. We sometimes say it out of habit and not out of the heart. Love is a choice, much more than a feeling. When we think of a marriage or relationship, we tend to mix our feelings with love. Love is easy when everything is going well. There will be good days, and not so good days, but our love should not be turned on and off like a light switch. Once we have found that special someone to be with and have committed to them, we must choose to let love be more than just a feeling. When we add cherish to the mix of love, that takes everything to a whole new level. Cherish means to protect and care for someone lovingly. When we chersh someone, we want to protect them, respect them, and hold them dear to our hearts. Think about a man who loves and cherishes an old car that he took the time and money to restore. Once restored, he is going to do everything he can to show it off and to protect it. He will be very careful how he treats it so it will not get damaged. Even during the restoration process, he is very careful and particular about how to go through this process and not settling for just anything, especially cheap parts. That's how we should consider our personal relationships.

Cherishing the one we love, as opposed to just loving them, adds value and deepens the relationship. It is a constant reminder of God's grace to us as we are renewed by the Holy Spirit. This will enable us to forgive, love, and look for new ways to bless them, even show grace in their shortcomings.

PRAYER:

Dear Father,

Thank you for the revelation of love and cherish. I pray that I will be committed to my relationship just as Christ was to the church. Continue to teach me new ways to love and cherish my spouse or love one. In Jesus Name. Amen.

SCRIPTURE FOCUS: Romans 12:10

"Be devoted to one another in love. Honor one another above yourselves."

AFFIRMING FOCUS:

I am committed to love my significant other. I am committed to cherish my significant other. I will find creative ways to keep the love alive in my relationship.

MY SPACE FOR REFLECTING

(IT IS WRITTEN)

DAY THIRTY

I GOT THE VICTORY!

It doesn't matter what we are going through, victory is available in Christ Jesus. He intends for us to live victorious lives. When we make Him Lord of our lives, we have gained the greatest victory of all, life over death. Living a victorious life means that we have turned all our cares and concerns over to God. **(I Peter 5:7)** declares that we are to cast all of our cares upon Him, for He cares for us. He is certainly equipped to handle every trial and tribulation that we can present to Him. When we think of victory, we may think about winning a battle or overcoming obstacles. In this life, we will definitely have hardships of some sort. Regardless if it's emotional, financial, physical or spiritual, we can face these conflicts knowing that God is on our side, and He will see us through. Jesus already won the victory when He took all the sins of the world to the cross. It's not enough to know that Jesus died for all of our sins, we must believe this in our hearts. In addition to believing, Jesus wants us to be prepared for the battles that we may face so they do not overtake us. Preparation for various trials and tribulations come by reading His word, praying, seeking His will, and putting on His armor. As we journey through life, we are guaranteed to make mistakes, experience hurt and pain, but we must keep fighting the good fight and pressing forward. The fight is fixed, and we come out victorious every time because we know who is fighting on our behalf. There must be constant fellowship with the Lord in order to live a victorious life. Even when we fall short, victory is ours!

PRAYER:

Dear Father,

You are my victory. I am trusting you to give me victory over every trial and tribulation that I am facing. Thank you, Jesus, for giving me victory through the cross. I pray that your peace covers me through difficult times. In Jesus Name. Amen.

SCRIPTURE FOCUS:

I Corinthians 15:57 "But thanks be to God, who gives us victory through our Lord Jesus Christ."

AFFIRMING FOCUS:

I walk in victory every day of my life because I know who is fighting on my behalf.

MY SPACE FOR REFLECTING

(IT IS WRITTEN)

DAY THRITY-ONE

I AM HIS LIGHT

Now, more than ever, is the time for us, His daughters, to be a light in this dark world. Being a light means to be bright and to illuminate. In other words, stand out. The bible is clear when it speaks about being sanctified and set apart from the world. The enemy wants to cast dark clouds across this entire earth, but those of us who believe and stand firm on God's work, know that He has called us out of darkness to His marvelous light **(I Peter 2:9)**. Darkness can be defined as the absence of light which can also be interpreted as the absence of God. Being the light in the earth goes far beyond doing good deeds. Yes, good deeds are essential and God is pleased when we do well for our fellow brothers and sisters, but as a reflection of the Creator, we should possess Christ-like qualities to shine for Him. Qualities like honesty, patience, positivity and graciousness are just a few. Of course all of the fruit of the Spirit; love, joy, peace, longsuffering, gentleness, goodness, faith, Meekness, and temperance are major Christ-like qualities that will shed light in darkness. Light is a sign that there is a source to the light. Jesus declares that He is the source of the light of the world. Whoever follows Him will not walk in darkness, but will have the light of life **(John 8:12)**. When people interact with us, it should be like an interaction with the Father. For we may be the only bible that they may read. In order for our light not to go out, we must stay connected to the source. We cannot compromise with the darkness. Without light, nothing living can survive.

PRAYER:

Dear Father,

Thank you for being the greatest example of light in the world. Help me to shine bright in these times of uncertainty with all of your Christ-like qualities. In Jesus Name. Amen.

SCRIPTURE FOCUS: II Corinthians 4:6

"For God, who said, Let light shine out of darkness, made his light shine in our hearts to give us light of the knowledge of God's glory displayed in the face of Christ."

AFFIRMING FOCUS:

I am the light reflecting Jesus Christ. I will display His qualities in this world of darkness.

MY SPACE FOR REFLECTING

(IT IS WRITTEN)

ABOUT THE AUTHORS:

Author Jamilla Robertson

Jamilla Robertson is best known as a minister of the gospel, motivational speaker, author, encourager, fiancé, mom, and a great friend to many. She is a single mother of two teenagers: Jamya (17) and Marti (15). Jamilla loves to spend time with her children, her girlfriends, and loves to date the love of her life, Darrell, whom she will marry soon.

Jamilla passionately believes that ministry starts ay home. She also devotes a lot of time to her women's group, ***Sisters, Let's Giv'em Something to Talk About.*** Her group meets on a monthly basis to encourage women to live a more excellent life, both spiritually and naturally. Jamilla hopes that her encouragement and inspiring messages will further push women to search within themselves to find out who they really are and for what reason they were put on this Earth, in the first place.

"Life" has taught her to be strong when faced with adversity, both mentally and spiritually. The Army taught her to be strong physically. Jamilla spent three years in the United States Army and three years in the National Guard, serving our country.

Because of the gift, talent, and ministry God intentionally placed on the inside of Jamilla, she WILL continue to inspire everyone that she encounters to keep ***givin'em something to talk about***, on a positive note, that is!

ABOUT THE AUTHORS

Author Sharonette Smart, DE

Sharonette Smart, born in Savannah, Georgia, feels that her greatest accomplishments are her four beautiful daughters: Zachoyia, Ciara, Amiya, Shaniya, and her grandson Author Noah Brooks.

Sharonette is the Founder and CEO of ***Single Mothers United of the World, Inc.***, a non-profit organization that supports single moms and their children. She is a Domestic Engineer, Evangelist, Entrepreneur, Impartation Messenger, Author, Real Estate Broker, Life Insurance Broker, Founder and CEO of SmartChoice Publishing Group, LLC, The Exit Plan, and The RIVERS. Sharonette is also a Literary Book Coach and Agent with SHERO Publishing Company and Team.

Sharonette's first book, ***The Load I Carry...Cast Your Cares!*** is a 31-Day Inspiration Devotional dedicated to single moms, which was birthed out of her own process and journey. Sharonette wanted to provide other Domestic Engineers with a resource that would encourage, empower them. She wants to inspire them to ***Live In Purpose,*** To never give up; and to never give in. Sharonette strives to encourage her readers to trust God, even when they can't feel Him, just know He's there.

Her motto is...

I Am My Sister's Keeper!
Together We Are Stronger!

Thank You Father for entrusting us, Your daughters, with this assignment. May this 31-Day journey and daily walk draw the reader closer to You, Father. Is our prayer.

~Daddy's Girls

AUTHOR CONTACTS

To contact Authors for speaking engagements, book signings, workshops, interviews, etc. You may contact them via the following:

Author Sharonette Smart

Email: info@sharonettesmart.com
FB: @AuthorSharonetteSmart
IG: @sharonette_

Author Jamilla S. Robertson

Email: jamillamotivatesu@gmail.com
FB: @jamilla.s.robertson
IG: @jamilla_givemsomethin2tlkabout

shero publishing

getpublished@sheropublishing.com

SHEROPUBLISHING.COM

shero publishing

getpublished@sheropublishing.com

SHEROPUBLISHING.COM

www.ingramcontent.com/pod-product-compliance
Lightning Source LLC
LaVergne TN
LVHW091002080826
845145LV00003B/1096